THERE IS little dispute ... that the Internet should continue as an open platform," notes the U.S. Federal Communications Commission. Yet in a curious twist of logic, the agency has moved to *discontinue* the legal regime yielding that open platform. In late 2010, it imposed "network neutrality" regulations on broadband-access providers, *both* wired and wireless. Networks cannot block subscribers' use of certain devices, applications, or services, or *unreasonably discriminate*, offering superior access for some services over others. The commission argues that such rules are necessary, as the Internet was designed to bar "gatekeepers." The view is faulty, both in its engineering claims and its economic conclusions. Networks routinely manage traffic and often bundle content with data transport precisely because such coordination produces superior service. Universities, for example, bar peer-to-peer services such as Skype; these nonprofit institutions harbor no hidden agendas and limit traffic simply to improve network performance for users. When "walled

[1]

gardens" emerged at AOL in 1995, with Japan's DoCoMo i-mode in 1999, or with Apple's iPhone in 2007, they often succeeded in disrupting old business models – attracting subscribers and providing golden opportunities for application developers. In many cases, these gardens have dropped their walls; others remain lush. This platform rivalry advances innovation and growth. A truly "open Internet" allows consumers, investors, and entrepreneurs to choose among many models, discovering efficiencies. The FCC mistakes the benefits of market processes for a planned industrial structure, imposing new rules to "protect" what evolved without it.

I. The New Network Neutrality Rules

The U.S. Federal Communications Commission, seeing the Internet as a fragile ecosystem under threat from opportunistic broadband providers, issued its "network neutrality" order on Dec. 23, 2010. The danger was intense and systemic. "Allowing gigantic corporations," wrote Commissioner Michael J. Copps, "to exercise unfettered control over Americans' access to the Internet not only creates risks to technological innovation and economic growth, but it poses a real threat to freedom of speech and the future of our democracy."

On Jan. 10, 2011, the FCC received its first official complaint – not against a "gigantic corporation" but an upstart wireless competitor providing innovative services, advanced technologies, and new options for low-income consumers.

The targeting of socially valuable entrepreneurship is hardly an accident. The regulatory effort – "preserving the free and open Internet," as the FCC frames it – mistakes the benefits of market rivalry for an architectural design. Competitive forces have driven firms to create vast data networks, continually upgrading their scope, speed, and quality. Cooperative agreements among these systems permit traffic to flow seamlessly through myriad gateways across the U.S. and around the world. Customers flock to these networks, eager to access a wondrous world of websites and online services, a thriving digital bazaar. This bountiful marketplace has emerged un-planned, unregulated, from the visions of technologists, the risks of venture capitalists, and the innovations of entrepreneurs, large and small.

The FCC mistakes the benefits of market processes for a planned industrial structure, imposing new rules to "protect" what evolved without it.

But that may change. Net neutrality (NN) rules restrict how companies may price and package computer network services. The rules prohibit bargains or bundles that are seen to discriminate among applications. Regulators see danger lurking in your broadband ISP, the cable TV system putting you online via a cable modem, or the telephone carrier connecting you via a digital subscriber line (DSL) or fiber-to-the-home (FTTH) networks. The operator, left to its own devices, is feared to maximize profits not just by taking your monthly subscription fee but by then skimming an unearned surcharge.

By "covertly blocking or degrading Internet traffic" to sites affiliated with rival content suppliers, the ISP is seen to be in position to favor those of its partners. There will be a fast lane on the Internet for those apps your "last mile" provider prefers – and a traffic jam for everyone else. The innovation in the garage does not enjoy the size, scope, or cash in the bank to buy its way in, discouraging grassroots innovation. "The harms that could result from threats to openness are significant and likely irreversible," warns the FCC.

Under the NN regime, rules generally mandate that ISPs not block access to (legal) websites or discriminate in the way traffic flows.

Customers make all the choices on a platform that treats all applications alike. Subscribers pay their ISP only once, and content providers do not pay that ISP at all. Conduits are open. The network is neutral. What's not to like?

II. Competition Destroys the Internet. *NOT*.

On Jan. 10, 2011, we found out. MetroPCS, the fifth-largest mobile network that competes with larger carriers by offering discount prices and short-term contracts, must defend itself. While its $40 a month "all you can eat" voice, text, and data plan does not accommodate video streaming or certain peer-to-peer applications, MetroPCS slipped in a bonus: free, unlimited YouTube videos.

Organizations favoring NN went ballistic. A petition to the FCC declared that the mobile provider favored YouTube over other video sites, creating a "walled garden" that would destroy the Internet. "The new service plans offered by MetroPCS give a preview of the future in a world without adequate protections for mobile broadband users," the complaint said. The filing could hardly be a surprise to regulators. The FCC order itself noted that "a major mobile broadband provider prohibits use of its wireless service for 'downloading movies using peer-to-peer file sharing services' and VoIP applications," referencing MetroPCS.

The complaint performs a great public service, revealing just how the commission's new regulations would "adequately protect mobile broadband users." In fact, MetroPCS possesses no market power. With 8 million customers, it is the country's fifth-largest mobile operator, less than one-tenth the size of Verizon. (*See Table 1*.) Under no theory could it force customers to patronize certain websites. It couldn't extract monopoly cash if it tried to.

Low-cost, prepaid plans offered by Metro-PCS are popular with price-sensitive customers and, particularly, with "cord cutters" whose only phone is wireless. Usage is intense. Voice minutes per month average about 2,000,

TABLE I.

TOP U.S. WIRELESS CARRIER METRICS, Q4 2010

Carrier	Subscribers (millions)	Revenue (millions)	Data % of Revenue	Revenue per Subscriber per Month
Verizon Wireless	102.246	$14,193	37.1%	$50.61
AT&T	95.536	$13,799	35.7%	$48.98
Sprint Nextel	49.650	$6,468	n/a	$47.87
T-Mobile	33.734	$4,615	27.5%	$46.59
MetroPCS	8.155	$972	n/a	$39.79
U.S. Cellular	6.072	$992	n/a	$54.37
Leap Wireless	5.518	$637	n/a	$38.14

more than double those of larger carriers. That implies that the average customer on the $40-per-month unlimited calling plan is paying just 2 cents per minute of use, *half* the U.S. average (which is itself the lowest among all developed economies). And unlimited texting, e-mail, and Web browsing are tossed in for free.

The $40 plan is inexpensively delivered via 2G (second-generation) technology. It is not technically broadband and has software and capacity issues. In general, voice-over-Internet protocol (VoIP) is not supported by handsets, and video streaming is not available on the network. The carrier deals with those limitations in three ways.

First, the $40-per-month price tag extends a fat discount. Unlimited everything can cost $120 on faster networks. Second, at a cost of a few billion dollars, it has deployed new 4G technology, offering both a $40 tier similar to the 2G product (no video streaming) but also a pumped-up version with video streaming, voice calls over Internet (via Skype), and everything else for $60 a month. *PC World* rates this 4G service "dirt cheap."

Third, to upgrade the 2G experience, Metro-PCS performed a little magic. Working with Google – the owner of YouTube – it figured out how to compress YouTube videos for delivery over the older network. This allowed the carrier to extend wildly popular YouTube content to its lowest-tier subscribers, who are offered unlimited downloads from the site.

Busted. In expanding its competitive package, MetroPCS favors YouTube – and that is said to violate neutrality. The pricing plans contain differences that "lack any engineering merit." But the special data-compression tweak improves customer service, providing *economic* merit. The confusion stems from the fact that network neutrality rules are developed via an *engineering* theory of Internet structure but are then slapped on *economic* activity. Hence, champions of net neutrality not only miss the efficiency of price competition, but the rules they advance do great violence to the rivalry that advances it. And benefits springing from the option for consumers to get more when they pay more are simply dismissed: "What if that $60 unlimited plan were $100? What about $600?" writes an author of the complaint. The NN position is that certain business plans render economic facts irrelevant.

In fact, MetroPCS *does* favor YouTube, one application among many. It folds in extra content with an Internet subscription to delight *its customers*. MetroPCS has no ownership interest in YouTube and receives no remuneration from Google. For MetroPCS to boost what its subscribers prefer is a real-world feature, not a bug.

Champions of net neutrality not only miss the efficiency of price competition, but the rules they advance do great violence to the rivalry that advances it.

Were MetroPCS to be accused, in an anti-trust proceeding, of *anticompetitive foreclosure* – what the NN rule is employed to pre-empt – the strategy, its implementation, and its effect would be spelled out. The case would require an explanation of how MetroPCS had acquired market power and was able to exploit it, harming consumers. This would consider how the carrier gained by favoring certain video sites. But this analysis would render the claim vacant; the carrier gains customers, who are happier, and nothing by thwarting YouTube's rivals. The foreclosure case collapses.

Helping customers is exactly what ISPS should be doing. This case may be resolved by a prompt dismissal, but its economics go far beyond. Innovators should need no defense in supplying superior choices. Productive alliances are typically *non-neutral*, advancing the interests of the partners who create them to the detriment of rival firms. Neither consumers nor the Internet are protected by rules hostile to cooperative efforts – even if money were to pass between firms, even when firms do enjoy market power – that expand outputs and lower prices. If network neutrality rules hit such targets, they will do far more to deter the "open Internet" than to preserve it.

III. Evidence-Based Public Policy

[The Commission's] processes should be open, participatory, fact-based, and analytically rigorous.
    – FCC Chair Julius Genachowski

There is no evidence that prior open Internet obligations have discouraged investment.
    – FCC 2010 NN order, par. 40

A. Methodology

It is clear to all participants in the NN debate that a key factor – perhaps the *most important* implication, in fact – relates to the impact of such regulations on investment decisions by network providers. Even should the rules succeed in suppressing anticompetitive conduct, the victory will prove Pyrrhic if infrastructure growth then slows. This is clearly a possibility, as the very point of the rules is to constrain ISPS, limiting their pricing and packaging decisions. When investors are told that they are less able to maximize returns and that they face additional regulatory overhead in justifying certain business models, the

---

Innovators should need no defense in supplying superior choices. Productive alliances are typically non-neutral, advancing the interests of the partners who create them to the detriment of rival firms.

---

first-order effect is a tax. As in the standard case, the tax will alter capital flows. Investors will shift marginal investment dollars to alternative opportunities. The case for NN relies on second-order impacts overcoming this effect.

The U.S. Department of Justice commented on the FCC's proposed rules, raising just this point. In dismissing the DOJ's concerns in a footnote, the FCC NN order states, "although the Department cautioned that care must be taken to avoid stifling infrastructure investment, it expressed particular concern about price regulation, which we are not adopting." The lack of seriousness in this response is striking. First, the commission dodges the substance of the argument by singling out one aspect of it – price regulation – and asserting that its plan avoids this path. Second, its response misunderstands the nature of the regulations, which do entail a form of "price regulation." Broadband operators cannot *price* certain applications on certain margins, as specified by regulators. Love them or hate them, the rules regulate prices.

The DOJ comment, targeting such constraints as particularly egregious, generally recommended an alternative regulatory approach: disclosure rules. The FCC order begins with such rules; the DOJ recommended ending there. Instead of NN rules, it advanced a policy initiative "promoting competition in broadband markets":

In practice, this does not mean striving for broadband markets that look like textbook markets of perfect competition, with many price-taking firms. That market structure is unsuitable for the provision of broadband services, which involve very substantial fixed and sunk costs. Rather, promoting competition is likely to take the form of enabling additional entry and expansion by wireless broadband providers, applying other appropriate policy levers, and spurring competition among broadband providers by improving the information available to consumers about the service offerings in their areas.

Notably absent: any form of price regulation. The stated reason, a chilling effect on incentives to expand physical infrastructure, is precisely why previous commissions declined to enact such controls on ISPs. For instance, the initial lobbying for "neutrality" rules governing broadband networks was launched in the

1990s by phone company GTE and dial-up ISP America Online. These interests, numerous advocacy groups, and highly regarded law professors argued that cable modem providers would inevitably bias customer choices, steering their subscribers to affiliated websites. The threat was purportedly severe, crushing innovation at the edge and deterring Internet growth. The proposed remedy was for FCC imposition of "open access" rules mandating cable TV systems rent broadband links to third-party providers at reasonable (regulated) rates. While the remedy focused on ISP access, the asserted "market failure" precisely tracks the current argument for network neutrality.

The FCC flatly rejected cable "open access" rules. In announcing the decision, then-FCC Chairman William Kennard put the point thusly: "We do not have a monopoly. We do not have a duopoly. We have a no-opoly." At an early stage of growth, it made no sense to presume that the market had already developed and was ready for regulation. More subtly, the statement was a stark admission: The reduction in industry growth dominated whatever static gains could be extended by encouraging more access to existing facilities. That tension continues to exist even as the emergent broadband-services market has matured.

This dynamism does not settle the issue. Advocates of network neutrality can and do argue that the advantages of mandated pricing rules enhance edge innovation and thereby overcome any disincentives imposed on investors in network facilities. But that is simply a hypothesis. It requires evidence to be compelling. Instead of empirical evidence, the FCC offers an observation: that great innovation has been produced at the network's edge. The agency then jumps to the conclusion that it imposes NN to protect these successful service and content providers from "blocking" or "discrimination." That confuses the very argument being made. If edge markets have flourished, it is in large measure because market forces have supported investment in infrastructure. That is an argument *against* new regulation. To argue that one is protecting the edge by newly regulating the core is to misunderstand the economic nature of complements. That applications like Google, Amazon, eBay, Twitter, and Facebook have emerged – from garages or dorm rooms to become giants of the Information Age – is precisely because broadband markets incentivize the creation of data-transport networks *and* accommodate the complements that make them valuable to customers.

The FCC assertion that "[t]here is no evidence that prior open Internet obligations have discouraged investment" turns out to be particularly easy to disprove, as research published in refereed economics journals has shown. (*See subsection C.*) That the commission imposed a grand new regulatory scheme while ignoring such evidence is in itself evidentiary.

B. *"Walled Gardens" of the Internet*

The Internet's founders intentionally built a network that is open, in the sense that it has no gatekeepers…

The network of networks – a diverse, inter-connected set of systems – spontaneously evolves. Economic structures are not planned administratively but emerge according to the interplay of competitive forces. Development relies heavily on investments made by network builders and application vendors who often coordinate their activities through contracts, partnerships, and standard-setting organiza-tions. Business models continuously change, as successful ideas earn the patronage of cus-tomers and profits for investors. This is not an exceptional pathway charted out in advance but a dynamic evolutionary process observed throughout the economy. It is instructive that Internet innovations are advanced by *entrepre-neurs*, seeded by *venture capitalists*, and taken mass-market by equity investors in *capital markets*.

As in other sectors, numerous components of Internet service are produced in parallel, often by firms that both compete and cooper-ate. The "'end-to-end' network architecture" the FCC cites as a special feature of computer networks is a general design principle that has never been offered as a fixed structure but as an approach to be applied "case by case." The packet-switched networks preceding the commercial Internet blocked access for private businesses as well as the general public, a stark violation of the "open Internet." These restrictions were appropriate, permitting funding agencies to achieve their objectives and so facilitating early advances in networking. The privatization of backbone networks, and the elimination of the ban on commercial access, unleashed more inclusive forms of organization – and the mass-market Internet. Evolving networks have routinely discriminated in pricing connections, in bundling services, and in transporting different types of traffic. "[I]t is well known that the end-to-end principle has been honoured more in the breach since the beginning of the commercial era."[1]

---

1 Craig McTaggart, *Was the Internet Ever Neutral?* Telecommunications Policy Research Conference paper (Sept. 30, 2006), p. 26. The passage cites to: Marjory S. Blumenthal & David D. Clark, *Rethinking the Design of the Internet: The End-to-End Arguments vs. the Brave New World*, in Benjamin M. Compaine & Shane Greenstein, *Communications Policy in Transition: The Internet and Beyond* (Cambridge: MIT Press, 2001), p. 91.

Economic incentives guide firms to typically specialize in either network transport or edge services. Modularity, in which rival firms provide complementary services without explicit coordination or integrated ownership, develops across many markets. Structures often migrate, however, from one architecture to another, as innovators test alternative forms of organization. Survivorship – Joseph Schumpeter's "creative destruction" – reveals effi - ciencies uncovered in the search of advantage.

The personal computer industry is a notable example. In the pre-PC universe, computers were (efficiently) produced by highly integrated firms. An IBM computer included IBM hardware bundled with IBM software. Components – from circuits to keyboards – were largely manufactured by IBM. As the industry developed, not only did PCs emerge to challenge and eventually upend the mainframe business, but the basic structure of production was radically altered. Software was unbundled from hardware, operating systems from applications, components from components. Thousands of specialized firms arose to do, in confined increments, what IBM had previously done as one. By the 1980s, major rivals to IBM, such as Dell Computers, were launched by assembling PCs with parts supplied by "the price system." Vertical integration had been replaced by a more "open" production network. This does not imply that more modularity is always preferred to less. Quite the obverse: The lesson is that efficient industrial structures change over time, and society benefits when we permit the experimentation that charts the path.

America Online

America Online (AOL) became an Internet powerhouse in the mid-1990s by distributing millions of easy-to-use sign-up disks and offer - ing a wide array of valuable content. Novice users flocked to the service; technical knowledge was unnecessary, and online access to the *New York Times* or proprietary (AOL-owned) features like The Motley Fool were a great lure. Bundling transport and edge apps

Efficient industrial structures change over time, and society benefits when we permit the experimentation that charts the path.

drew risk capital into marketing, intensifying Internet demand among previously lukewarm market segments and driving the World Wide Web to the mass market.

The firm's business structure violated "end-to-end." AOL was condemned as a "walled garden" that stifled consumer choice, application innovation, and Internet development. Today, it is routinely referenced as the rationale for the FCC's new net neutrality regulations. A recent editorial criticizing MetroPCS's service plans (prior to the formal complaint), analogized them to the old AOL: "Using walled gardens from the year 1999, the new

[MetroPCS] pricing forces customers to purchase the most expensive service tier to gain access to the real Internet, in essence making open Internet access a 'luxury tier'."

MetroPCS cannot, of course, "force customers to purchase the most expensive tier," but it does give them options. Not only does the price charged for full access to the "real Internet" compare favorably to choices offered by rival networks, but the opportunity for some consumers to buy a stripped-down version of the "real Internet" *expands* customer choice. The mechanistic vision of a fixed Internet structure obscures these basic economics. Ken Auletta's 2009 book *Googled: The End of the World as We Know It*, offers some historical detail worth noting:

> *Because AOL later went into a tailspin, it's often forgotten how dominant the company was. Webheads would sneer that using AOL was "the Internet on training wheels." Yet it was AOL's user-friendliness that helped popularize the web — and which attracted 34 million paid subscribers in 2002.*

The end of integrated ISPs – not only AOL but CompuServe, Prodigy, @Home and many others – came not because of "end-to-end" design but from unregulated competitive forces: When online content markets grew, efficiencies rendered by the integrated ISP faded. Perhaps market evolution will take another turn. Indeed, AOL's recent purchase of the Huffington Post, a news and opinion website launched in 2005, for $315 million, is a bet that the "walled garden" may yet have a pulse. It would be silly to allege that the AOL-HuffPo deal threatens to destroy the openness of the Internet. But such an implication is drawn from the FCC rationale for imposing network neutrality rules on broadband ISPs.

Apple iPhone

The mobile marketplace is a wondrous laboratory. Launched barely three decades ago, it is already the premier industry of the communications sector, disrupting fixed-network dominance, revolutionizing economies in the developing world, and bringing an array of lifestyle changes that presage enormous improvements in industrial efficiency, public safety, social networking, and health services. At the center of this social storm sits the mobile carrier.

Traditionally, wireless networks exercised a fair degree of vertical integration. Network operators purchased technology, base stations, and handsets from third-party providers, maintaining a broad control over the devices and applications that accessed their systems. A Verizon Wireless customer might buy a Motorola or LG handset and then use it to access base stations built by Ericsson or Lucent, all using CDMA algorithms developed by Qualcomm. These radios, this network infrastructure, the spectrum through which signals traveled, and the handset applications were all coordinated by the carrier.

Traditionally, mobile devices have been tightly tied to a particular mobile network. Customers had to purchase the handset that was associated with the network, and vice versa; the choice of network provider drove the choice of devices available.[2]

These "walled gardens" grew and prospered. But they have recently been upended, displaced by new "gardens" both walled and unfenced. Killer wireless applications arose from handset innovations and the platforms organized around them. Enterprise users, in particular, clamored for business devices to aid productivity. The most successful pioneer – the Blackberry, a product of Canadian Research in Motion – gained an independent following across rival networks. The center of gravity began to shift. When Apple's iPhone launched in 2007, it was linked to the Apple App Store. Software developers flocked to the

---

2 Stuart Taylor and Scott Puopol, *Leaving the Walled Garden: How Mobile Operators Can Survive in an Open World*, Cisco Internet Business Solutions Group White Paper (Oct. 2, 2008): http://www.cisco.com/web/about/ac79/docs/wp/Open_Mobile_POV_100208_FINAL.pdf.

new market. Seemingly overnight, hundreds of thousands of new applications were available for download straight to the phone, not through the carrier. Tectonic plates lurched. The smartphone revolution – joined by Google's Android platform, the Microsoft-Nokia alliance, and others – was on.

New structures formed, and they are not "open end-to-end." In fact, Apple's iconic wireless innovation both displaced, and replicated, existing industry models. That fact greatly alarmed champions of network neutrality. The iPhone is "iPhony," wrote Columbia Law School Professor Tim Wu. "If Apple wanted to be 'revolutionary,'" wrote Wu, "it would sell an unlocked version of the iPhone that, like a computer, you could bring to the carrier of your choice." Instead, Apple chose AT&T as its exclusive network and "forced" customers to use the App Store for software downloads.

Consumers paid the critique no mind. By year-end 2010, Apple had sold 20 million iPhones, a runaway consumer success. It is bizarre that critics would cite Apple's entrepreneurship as an attack on market innovation. The claim is that only a device that downloads any and all mobile applications, and runs on any network, is efficient. This reflects the theory that *vertical integration* is tantamount to *vertical foreclosure*, a clear misreading of the economics of industrial organization. As Stanford economist Bruce Owen explains:

> *While there is no shortage of theoretical models in which vertical integration may be harmful, most such models have restrictive assumptions and ambiguous welfare predictions — even when market power is assumed to be present. Empirical evidence that vertical integration or vertical restraints are harmful is weak, compared to evidence that vertical integration is beneficial — again, even in cases where market power appears to be present.*

Ronald Coase found long ago that firms continually explore ways to reduce costs and increase productivity by *expanding or contract-*

ing in scope. In general, companies extend their boundaries to produce additional inputs or complements when they can outperform independent suppliers. Every firm is vertically integrated to some degree, and every firm is vertically limited on some margins. The "walled garden" of Apple embeds Apple's Mac operating system on iPhones and limits phones to applications downloaded from the App Store. But processors, radios, and mem-

---

It is bizarre that critics would cite Apple's entrepreneurship as an attack on market innovation.

---

ory chips are purchased from suppliers; wide-area network connectivity is supplied (via contract) by a mobile carrier; and thousands of independent software developers write the programs approved for sale at the App Store, splitting revenues with Apple.

No particular industry structure is categorically superior to all others. What works best for consumers is a competitive process in which firms vie to discover preferred packages and pricing menus. When suppliers compete for inputs, buyers, and capital, a sophisticated balance obtains. Business models imposed by regulators – not so much.

Apple could have launched its phone as an "open" platform on rival networks. Indeed, Apple has often (as in Australia) produced the iPhone for multiple carriers. In 2011, it began selling iPhones in the U.S. on Verizon's, as well as AT&T's, network. Apple chose to create an ecosystem with a relatively high degree of vertical control in its iPhone App Store, ensuring product quality, ease of use across devices (iPods, iPod Touches, iPhones, iPads), and brand identification. That branding itself delivers value to consumers, conveying information about quality, functionality, and compatibility.

Competing models have arisen. Responding to the success of Apple's "proprietary" platform, Google launched a distinct alternative in late 2007. The Android operating system is licensed by Google, without fee, to mobile-device makers such as Samsung, HTC, and Motorola. The Android Marketplace allows phone users easy access to apps offered by developers without the much tighter approval process administered in the App Store. (But both Google and Apple take a substantial cut of revenues.) Android has grown at a frantic pace, becoming the world's leading smart-phone operating system by year-end 2010. Nothing in the "walled garden" planted by Apple could pre-empt this outcome. Indeed, it inspired it.

NTT DoCoMo

Perhaps an equally impressive burst of inno-vation was launched in 1999 by Japan's DoCoMo. The i-mode handset, exclusively provided by the network, enabled easy access to e-commerce sites. The advance was remark-able, in that networks did not then feature broadband capabilities, nor were there more than a handful of Japanese Internet subscribers (fixed or mobile). DoCoMo, the wireless arm of the erstwhile state telecommunications monopolist NTT, blazed entirely new ground – as an entrepreneurial "gatekeeper."

The carrier supplied cellphone users with Web access optimized for wireless. Content providers, to be featured on the preferred menu, paid a cut to DoCoMo (9 percent of revenue), which billed end users. Application developers abided by strict rules as to how they designed websites and interacted with customers. Economist Len Waverman, dean of the business school at the University of Calgary, wrote that DoCoMo initiated three significant controls: limiting prices charged by independent vendors, showing customers their charges for content in real time as incurred, and restricting bandwidth-hogging applications.

Rejecting "neutrality," i-mode proved to be a rousing – and disruptive – success, attracting more than 35 million subscribers by mid-2003. DoCoMo's mobile rivals responded with managed Web platforms of their own. The wireless Web became the dominant form of Internet access in Japan. Today, customers choose from bountiful, competing gardens. By consensus, Japanese wireless data markets are the most developed anywhere in the world.

C. Broadband Regulation Slows Network Development: The Evidence

The FCC asserts that net neutrality regulation will promote investment:

Restricting edge providers' ability to reach end users, and limiting end users' ability to choose which edge providers to patronize, would reduce the rate of innovation at the edge and, in turn, the likely rate of improvements to network infrastructure. Similarly, restricting the ability of broadband providers to put the network to innovative uses may reduce the rate of improvements to network infrastructure.

The FCC has examined no systematic economic evidence supporting this belief. That is seen in the NN order's citation of a research paper by University of Chicago economist

Austan Goolsbee in response to experts who have pointed out their omission:

In addition to the examples of actual misconduct that we provide ... the Goolsbee Study provides empirical evidence that cable providers have acted in the past on anti-competitive incentives to foreclose rivals, supporting our concern that these and other broadband providers would act on analogous incentives in the future. We thus disagree that we rely on "speculative harms alone" or have failed to adduce "empirical evidence."

This passage is remarkable in four respects. First, while arguing against the proposition, it

---

What works best for consumers is a competitive process in which firms vie to discover preferred packages and pricing menus.

---

implicitly concedes that its parade of horribles is not tantamount to economic evidence. It merely posits "speculative harms" and, to defend the practice, advances one study that purportedly supports its position. This selectively ignores numerous studies that find vertical integration in cable television to be pro-competitive, and the large body of evidence that finds vertical integration to be widely efficient throughout the economy.

Second, the commission does not cite any research evaluating *broadband* services, offering only Goolsbee's 2007 analysis of how cable TV systems select basic cable channels. This is a stunning concession: The agency could not find a single scholarly study supporting its policy position in the broadband market.

Third, the cited research does not examine the *effects of regulation.* It is well known that, in proposing government controls on economic behavior, it is insufficient to assert "market failure." It is crucial to establish that new rules would be salubrious, increasing consumer welfare. Of course, all regulations have costs and consequences (intended and unintended) of their own, so a careful balancing is part and parcel of the analysis. The commission referenced no research establishing that such regulation has been, or will be, effective.

Finally, the FCC simply misreads the research it cites. The order states that Goolsbee shows "that MVPDS excluded networks that were rivals of affiliated channels for anticompetitive reasons." That is incorrect. The Goolsbee paper claimed to find that in markets where market rivalry was less intense – with competition measured by the level of direct broadcast satellite (DBS) penetration in the surrounding geographic market – cable TV operators tended to favor more of their own programming. This relationship was key to revealing a situation in which an operator uses its own programming because it is more efficient, rather than a case in which the operator is *anticompetitively* foreclosing rivals. (*See http://www.arlingtoneconomics.com/studies/Paper. FCC.Filed.10.22.07.pdf.*)

In Goolsbee's model, as competition increased, the favoritism disappeared. As estimated, the critical values for the crossover point – the DBS penetration level at which cable TV systems stop discriminating against rival network programming – generally lie *below actual* DBS penetration levels. Hence, what Goolsbee shows, in its own terms, is that bias has been erased by market rivalry. That is, cable TV operators *are not* "excluding networks that were rivals of affiliated channels for anticompetitive reasons." There are several reasons to doubt Goolsbee's analysis on other grounds, but the FCC's misinterpretation of its results renders the analysis moot. The commission's one citation to empirical research – even ignoring the fact that it is inapt and irrelevant – falls flat. Its order presents no empirical support for the proposition that cable systems are foreclosing rivalry, let alone that broadband regulation will likely prove pro-consumer.

There is, however, persuasive empirical research that is on point. Some U.S. broadband services have been regulated and then deregulated, with rival networks treated differently under the rules. This allows for an analysis that considers the relevant question: Do federal mandates to enforce "open" broadband networks tend to enhance consumer welfare? This query is answered in Thomas W. Hazlett & Anil Caliskan, "Natural Experiments in Broadband Regulation," 7 *Review of Network Economics* (Dec. 2008), 460–80.

As noted above, "open access" regulations – sought by various interests beginning in the late 1990s – would have required cable TV operators to offer rival firms the use of their broadband networks on regulated terms and conditions. The argument paralleled the one made for net neutrality. While regulators stood firm, denying multiple petitions for mandated access to cable systems, legacy telecommunications network controls were enforced, and then abandoned, for rival broadband services offered by phone companies. This permits economic analysis of the differences observed in the marketplace following distinct policy variations.

While cable modem (CM) services have always been unregulated, "open access" rules were initially applied to DSL broadband services delivered by local exchange carriers. These permitted phone-company rivals (commonly called "data competitive local exchange carriers," or dCLECs) to lease broadband connections at regulated rates. Because dCLECs could share the copper wires already serving voice customers, using the high-frequency portion of the line, some states set "line sharing" fees at very low levels (some at zero). This policy was pre-empted by a rule change in February 2003, however, when the FCC ended "line sharing" as a pricing model. Leasing costs jumped significantly, dCLEC services were largely eliminated, and "open access" for telco/DSL networks effectively ended. In August 2005, the deregulation was extended when formal access rules were stripped away, putting CM and DSL networks under the same regime. This pattern yields three distinct broadband policy periods, summarized in Table 2.

TABLE 2. THREE REGIMES IN BROADBAND

Period	Cable Modems	Telecoms/DSL
before Q1 2003	unregulated	regulated with "line sharing" obligation
Q1 2003 to Q3 2005	unregulated	regulated but no "line sharing"
Q1 2005 to present	unregulated	deregulated

The theory that broadband network regulation efficiently prevents anticompetitive actions by ISPs yields distinct implications. The protection of innovation on such networks, via specific rules, aims to make such networks more advantageous for application vendors and more valuable to consumers. These effects should evince themselves in subscriber levels, which encompass impacts from both investments to expand and upgrade networks, and decisions by consumers to purchase services. Either effect correlates positively with subscribership.

Examining the subscribership metric on a quarterly basis, 1999 through 2006, allows us to test the implications of the theory. The basic hypothesis is that a network subjected to "open access" mandates will gain subscribers relative to networks without such regulatory protections, all else equal. Of course, there are many other differences between cable modem

---

The FCC could not find a single scholarly study supporting its policy position in the broadband market.

---

and DSL services, including technological factors, service attributes, and historical build-out levels, in addition to the differential regulatory mandates. That makes it important to compare subscriber growth through time as regimes are changing: The ratio of subscriber growth (across technologies) is predicted to respond accordingly. It is also advisable to adjust for factors that might shift the observed ratio due to factors other than regulatory changes – say, shifts in technology.

The Hazlett-Caliskan study follows this format. It first examines the contemporaneous subscriber growth in U.S. cable and telephone network broadband services through three periods. From the first quarter of 1999 (1999-1) through the last quarter of 2002 (2002-4), the telephone networks used to supply DSL services were heavily regulated under "line sharing" rules. During this period, unregulated cable modem subscribers consistently outnumbered DSL subscribers by about 2 to 1. In 2003-1, however, a sharp deregulatory break occurred when the FCC ended line-sharing rules. Almost immediately, total DSL subscriber growth surged both absolutely and relative to cable modem subscriber growth. By 2005, quarter-on-quarter DSL subscriber additions were outstripping cable modem gains. Then in August 2005, the FCC extended DSL deregulation, placing DSL broadband services at parity with cable. In this last period, 2005-3 through 2006-4, DSL subscriber growth continued to spurt relative to CM subs.

The magnitude of the DSL growth increase following deregulation is seen in Figure 1. Were the DSL subscribership pattern through 2002 to extend through year-end 2006 (2006-4), there would have been about 15 million subscribers. The actual number of subscribers, however, was more than 25 million, an increase some *65 percent above trend*. Over the same period, and using the same forecast methodology, cable modem growth also ticked up, but by just 11 percent.

It is possible that some exogenous factor drove DSL into catch-up mode during the post-deregulation period. The leading candidate would be a shift in technology. Perhaps digital subscriber lines became better, or cheaper, because of changes in global telecom equipment markets rather than FCC rules. To test for this possibility, Hazlett-Caliskan models U.S. DSL subscriber growth as a function of

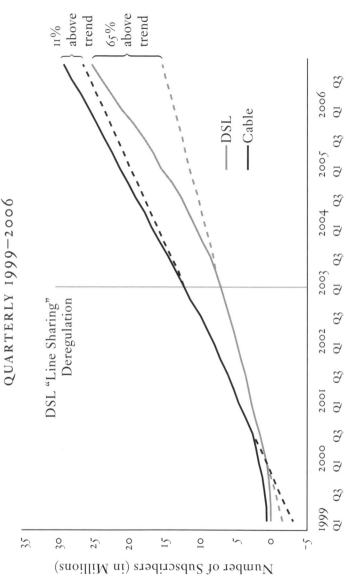

FIGURE 1. U.S. CABLE MODEM AND DSL SUBSCRIBERS, QUARTERLY 1999–2006

same period (a) U.S. cable broadband sub-scriber growth; (b) Canadian cable modem subscriber growth; and (c) Canadian DSL sub-scriber growth. DSL subscriber growth is then evaluated econometrically. If marketplace changes are favoring DSL over cable modem services during this time, the shifts seen in U.S. broadband services should also be observed in Canada. Canada features broad-band markets structured similarly to the U.S. in terms of rivalry between cable modems and DSL. If other factors (beyond U.S. regulatory changes) are influencing the "broadband race," then those factors should be evident in the Canadian market. Including cable modem and DSL subscriber levels from Canada should then explain the changing ratio of broadband subscribers in the U.S.

Regression analysis indicates, however, that Canadian broadband growth does not explain the results in the United States. DSL sub-scriber growth skyrockets after "open access" mandates are removed, and it does so only in the U.S. These market experiments show that broadband regulation substantially impacts network growth – *negatively*. Such outcomes, strongly buttressed by the development of fiber-to-the-home services in the U.S. only after regulators barred "open access" mandates in 2004, provide direct evidence against the FCC's hypothesis that regulatory measures to limit "gatekeepers" advance Internet growth. Regulators have simply ignored the data – a curious path to "evidence-based policy."

IV. The Antitrust Alternative to "Network Neutrality"

In 2008, the FCC attempted to sanction Comcast for degrading certain peer-to-peer services (useful for downloading movies) used by its broadband subscribers. The foray was rebuffed by the D.C. Circuit Court of Appeals, which determined that the commission was operating beyond its congressional charter. The court did not get to the substance of the FCC's extralegal actions. That is a pity.

Comcast claimed that it was managing its

network to limit congestion, seeking to protect the great bulk of its customers from traffic generated by a few. If true, such actions would "preserve a free and open Internet," not undermine it. The commission, however, saw the country's largest cable-system operator as blocking Web videos to stop its customers from cannibalizing the operator's video-on-demand (VOD) revenues. No evidence was presented to support this proposition. In fact, Comcast's broadband (CM) revenues dominated its VOD revenues on the order of 20 to 1. Degrading the former (which generates massive cash flow) to protect the latter (a relatively trivial profit center) requires some explanation. Moreover, Comcast's aggressive billion-dollar network upgrades – delivering faster and faster speeds for its CM subscribers (today, Comcast offers over 100 Mbps, ultrafast broadband, to all of the 40 million homes it passes) – constitute a curious way to block Comcast's cable TV customers from accessing Web video content. These and other facts present a tall order for a theory of anticompetitive foreclosure. Yet beyond the speculation that Comcast may have acted to sabotage competition and had "unduly squelched" broadband usage, the FCC made no attempt to delineate how Comcast's *efficient* interest in improving connectivity for all its customers had given way to *inefficient* measures thwarting competitive rivalry.

Networks with no possible anticompetitive

Market experiments show that broadband regulation substantially impacts network growth – negatively.

---

motive, no fear of cannibalization or lost profits, "duly squelch" all the time. University IT administrators frequently ban peer-to-peer services outright, a far more severe approach than that undertaken by Comcast or other commercial networks. Skype, an application that helps users make cheap voice calls around the world, is seriously hurt by the practice. Yet its peer-to-peer format can tax bandwidth, reducing network access for other users. It is efficient for IT administrators to manage traffic, which is why their institutions direct them to do so. That such network-management practices create controversy is not surprising. Users are in conflict, and administrative choices favor different parties. To fail to make such choices would not make the network "open" or "neutral." It would *discriminate* in favor of certain (bandwidth intensive) applications and/or those in which latency (caused by network congestion) is not so much of a problem. While the light flashes green for some, it flashes red for others.

Comcast's effort to smooth network-traffic flows was resolved not by regulation but by simple fixes negotiated privately. The company's disclosure policies were adjusted to better inform subscribers as to how network-management practices would be applied.

Comcast then instituted explicit "bandwidth caps" that limited how much data a subscriber may send or receive. This is a proactive measure undertaken by operators – Comcast's having been followed by many other broadband providers – to reinforce network-management efforts. In its actions that led to the FCC action, Comcast appears to have clumsily engaged measures that were not fully spelled out, even internally, in order to prevent traffic jams. Now broadband providers are largely committed to "duly squelch" all data bits that exceed specified plan limits. While many net neutrality advocates praised the FCC's Comcast ruling before it was overturned (Harvard law professor Lawrence Lessig told the commission that it had made it "clear that those who wish to profit from the Internet do so without harming the Internet"), this is hardly what the campaign for net neutrality claimed as an objective.

The singular responsibility of a regulatory agency is to conscientiously evaluate the social costs and benefits of its actions. The FCC has dispensed with such overhead, simply postulating a categorical rule and then executing ad hoc interventions. Its initial effort was overturned by the courts; the next – the December 2010 NN order – may soon be. No matter. There exists a body of law that, with more than a century of practice and precedent, is widely used to detect and police anticonsumer conduct. Those most familiar with the nature of competition, the economics of networks, and the institutions of regulation offer a consensus on the superiority of antitrust law as a framework for policing the "open Internet." Such proceedings, imperfect though they are, require evidence, economic analysis, and a verdict on consumer welfare. As we stumble in the midst of duly and unduly squelches, this policy argument will become more and more compelling.

First American edition published in 2011 by Encounter Books,
an activity of Encounter for Culture and Education, Inc.,
a nonprofit, tax exempt corporation.
Encounter Books website address: www.encounterbooks.com

Manufactured in the United States and printed on
acid-free paper. The paper used in this publication meets
the minimum requirements of ANSI/NISO Z39.48–1992
(R 1997) (*Permanence of Paper*).

FIRST AMERICAN EDITION

LIBRARY OF CONGRESS CATALOGING-IN-PUBLICATION DATA

Hazlett, Thomas W.
The fallacy of net neutrality / Thomas W. Hazlett.
p.   cm.
ISBN-13: 978-1-59403-592-0 (pbk. : alk. paper)
ISBN-10: 1-59403-592-X (pbk. : alk. paper)
1. Internet—Social aspects—United States. 2. Internet—
Government policy—United States. 3. Digital divide—
United States. 4. Broadband communication systems—
United States. I. Title.
HM851.H396 2011
303.48'330973—dc23
2011018852

10 9 8 7 6 5 4 3 2 1